Praise for
Dawn of this Hunger

"*Dawn of this Hunger* is a startling literary achievement. Nothing in the work of any contemporary poet prepares us for the impact of these poems. To the passion and exactness with which Sally Read evokes the story of the Incarnation—from conception to resurrection—is added, in poem after poem, against all expectation, ways in which so many of the details of that story, both great and small, are found to be resonant with our own lives, our own fears and desires, our own hunger. At one moment, informed by a transcendent lyricism, at another by a bold, uncompromising directness of thought and expression—these bright, sharp lyrics are as down-to-earth as they are visionary. They peel away, as well, the dull varnish of false sentiment, the false colors which have, for centuries, all too often obscured the true and living image of Mary and of her Son. In that sense, we can say, the work is revelatory."—
PAUL MURRAY, OP, author of *A Journey with Jonah: The Spirituality of Bewilderment*

"I am indebted to Sally Read for the moments of stunning beauty she has brought to me in her verse. Breath-taking, pause-making, gratitude-giving, wonder-filling, contemplation-inducing, soul-dilating. To borrow from her own image-hoard, her voice is as fresh as 'early morning air, pure as vodka.' Her poems are truly words distilled into spirit."—
JOSEPH PEARCE, author of *Literature: What Every Catholic Should Know*

"From 'The Quickening' to the poet's raw reality in her 'Passion' offerings, to the stunning description of 'The Mother' (just to name a few), the poetry of Sally Read transports the reader to poignant destinations. Through her imaginative wordcraft we perceive the past as evermore present. We are suddenly witnesses with a conscience as 'tender as a sunburned neck,' to quote Flannery O'Connor. *Dawn of this Hunger* by Sally Read will thrill the reader."—BARBARA MCGUIGAN, Host of EWTN's *The Good Fight*

"These poems wrestle with, and partake of, the incredible. Steeped as they are in awe, they are doubly engaged as they grapple viscerally and sensitively with the Christian mysteries. Sally Read enters into situations that are at once personal occasions and episodes of sanctified lore. Rarely does a poet take on such quiet, persistent enormities as are present in these poems. They are devout avowals made before presences that have shaken her being to its spiritual core."—BARON WORMSER, Poet Laureate of Maine, 2000–2005

"This gorgeous, lyrical collection of poems by Sally Read glows with luminous insight. *Dawn of this Hunger* offers a profound yet accessible series of meditations on the life of Christ, sensitively reimagining the perspectives of those who knew him, intercalated with a shimmering series of more personal reflections. Christ's mother figures strongly as Read dwells on the embodied mystery of her unique maternal calling. The book's many voices reflect the light and shadow of our own natures. Throughout, language is beautifully woven, 'like honeycomb' ('The Hermit'), and each poem offers its own light, 'like buds on the stark branches of our prayer' ('The Quickening'). This is resonant, contemplative, truthful, and frequently joyful poetry."—SARAH LAW, author of *Thérèse: Poems*

Dawn of this Hunger

Dawn of the Vampire

Dawn
of this
Hunger

Poems
by
Sally Read

First published in the USA
by Second Spring
an imprint of Angelico Press
© Sally Read 2021

For information, address:
Angelico Press
169 Monitor St.
Brooklyn, NY 11222
www.angelicopress.com

pbk: 978-1-62138-792-3
cloth: 978-1-62138-793-0

Cover image:
Odilon Redon, *Reflection*, 1900–1905, pastel
Cover design:
Michael Schrauzer

Preface

The poems in this collection were written after my rather dramatic conversion from atheism to Catholicism: this took place in 2010, in the space of nine months. I had moved to live by the sea near Rome, and soon came into contact with a young priest who had fled Ukraine after fighting corruption there. He would quickly become my instructor in the mysteries of the Catholic faith. The full story is recounted elsewhere, but one image from those days comes to mind as I introduce this book. We were waiting in the icy cold for a train to Rome, where we would confirm the arrangements for my confirmation, when we suddenly confessed to one another that neither of us had any idea about the shape of the future. In terms of my writing, I felt as though I were leaving everything behind.

I was already a poet, having published three books of poetry. My reputation, such as it was, was that of a feisty young woman unafraid of writing about the body and sex. I intuited that when I became Catholic the audience for my poems would change. I didn't even know if I would write poetry at all anymore: my conversion meant that my very being was undergoing an almost harsh clarification. The priest was also at the threshold of a bold move: he had left his monastic order and very recently established his own hermitage. On the train that day, empty fields and silver sea hovering beside us, I knew an uncertainty unlike any other I have known. But we both seemed paradoxically free from fear.

It was partly this uncertainty that made me tell the new hermit, Father Gregory, that I would be his hermitage's 'poet in residence'. Now a Catholic, I thought it would help me to write for a purpose, to have a focus, and also, in a sense, a shelter. That was the beginning of these poems. They were written with no overall plan, but their inception was usually related to scripture or feasts. Over the years, pieces emerged in the voices of, or about, Saint

Anne, Saint Elizabeth, Saint Peter, Saint Mary Magdalene—and others—but especially Our Lady. In the course of writing I realized that all our own stories, our grief and our joys, fit into the shapes of the events and emotions in Christ's life and the lives of those surrounding him. We can find refuge in him precisely because of that fit.

The span of these poems reaches from the conception of Mary, until the Resurrection and beyond. 'Beyond' because Christ's presence, of course, extends far before and beyond his earthly ministry; and the last poems in this book reflect something of that presence directly in me and in the hermitage. Throughout I have also woven in pieces (in italics) that are addressed directly to God: these were written alongside the central narrative thread.

I make one last observation as I bring this collection together. For all the people from Scripture and Tradition whose perspective I explore I never write in Christ's voice, or from his point of view. As Christ's story unfolds there is a sense of drawing close to a white-hot fire, or standing at the edge of a hurricane. In this, our Mother's unique role as guide has been brought home to me strongly. I have often walked as close as I could to her, in her hiddenness and unsurpassable love, to get as close as possible to her Son. And in fact she, of anyone aside from God, occupies the greatest number of poems.

Finally, I would like to dedicate this book to the Hermitage of the Three Holy Hierarchs, its protector the Theotokos, and its mission of preaching, teaching and prayer.

SALLY READ
November 2021
Year of Saint Joseph

Every book depends to some extent on the wise eyes, encouragement and support of others. I would particularly like to thank Father Paul Murray OP and Hieromonk Gregory Hrynkiw for their patience and kindness over the years as I've tried to give voice to this new faith.

Acknowledgements are due to the editors of the following publications where some of these poems first appeared: *The Catholic Herald*, *Magnificat*, and online at The Poetry Room (www.integratedcatholiclife.org), *Cheminons Avec Marie Qui Défait les Noeuds* (https://blog.gingko-editions.fr/), and The Asketerion (www.asketerion.com). *Anne: The Coming of the Immaculate* and *The Quickening* were broadcast on Radio Maria England in Advent 2020. A small number of images in the italicized pieces began life as haiku that I was commissioned to write for *Off the Beaten Track*, Boatwhistle Books, London, 2016.

CONTENTS

Silence

Early morning air,
pure as vodka.
It blurs the emerald pines.
We are nourished
by darkness and silence,
but still unprepared.
The cool fields wake,
astounded. Every day
I know you again—
from nothing.

Anne: The Coming of the Immaculate

At times prayer is wordless, but it fills
the empty night as water fills a lake
with its own meaning. I pray to break
this body with a child, for my taut pelvis
to open and ache its tight basketwork
apart; to *yield*. Sometimes I sense God
in the darkness—like a heavy leaning
at the door—always with an inexplicable
tenderness in how he does not burst in.
Perhaps he would break me if he did,

so waits instead to pour into my own undoing—
so just when I would moan, *It's done!*
that life did not go well, *Perfection* rests in me,
and I expand, like wood ticking in the sun.

From before first light
she prays. The sea
silvers at the dawn's touch;
darkens with a cloud.
So she mirrors you.

Annunciation

The girl's so still, a clutch of starlings
might roost in her. Her thirteen years,
and more, are recollected in his gaze,
as the purple-blue of rosemary is lost
in what is happening. Steady as earth
she is, and soft: like turf penetrated
by deep hooks of roots. How he watched her,
from the empty dawn of before-all-time.

No gunshot would startle that stillness,
or even make the birds around her fly.
A prayer deep enough for God himself
to tread. As though she were earth and he
the weightless footfall, unused to gravity
and human flesh, sighing into her consent.

What the Sparrow Saw

In the long afternoon, dull with expected sunlight,
is it possible that a bird nearby would not be changed,
at its scorched wingtip or in its jagged gaze,
by what it witnessed? Would it have seen the angel,
or just the staggered girl holding her own hands?
Would she have been so still that he rested
for a moment on her arm (like a winter branch, but soft)?
Or would he have jittered, flitted at the immense bodiless
made present (like a sunset on the doorstep,
a tsunami in the barn)? And if his breast feathers
were warmed, shaken harder by his miniscule heart;
if his eyes contained, then, a moment's intense knowledge
at what was near, or even a crazed bird-madness,
what deep hope for me as I kneel before your Presence?

Afterwards

It wasn't just one afternoon, it never is.
And though the angel's face and legs,
portentous hands, may not have come again,
she must have knelt then
many times, just where she was,
weighed by the miracle within,

and seen against low sun the jasmine
black as cut-out paper silhouettes,
and water in a pitcher
darkening with its load of night,
like ink to soak the world in;
her prayer, darkening

to wordless shapes; her heart
steeped in love so deep
its edges bleed; her skin become
alert, like something
listening—
the tightening, tender boundary
between us and him.

Elizabeth

...when the voice of your greeting came to my ears,
the child in my womb leaped for joy (Luke 1, 44)—

he leapt like a fish
up to sunlight, grasping
the winged words,
as if he were my ears, or that part of me
that knows God,
and I was lifted
with him—
        so that I seemed,
for a moment, taken
to pure emptiness—
as though in a field, say,
starlings dropped down
into furrows
and the white sky aching
its absence, a place
where the mind
stops tarrying
with voices, bustle,
and breathes, suddenly,
at the precipice
of God—
        just this, an opening
to presence, a sense of the edge
of his silence that makes us sing
into the deep for reply—

                                   the child
leapt in me like a fish
and sunk back,
clutching tight this shining,
incomparable song
to the dark waters
of our waiting.

Magnificat

That day I think dark clouds
were slashed by flecks

of one blackbird's song—
clear, as though he sang

in a shut cupboard—
and the sky shook as though

its distant walls would fall.
Then there was human song—

the only way those words could come—
and 'The child leapt in her womb'.

A new flame spilled and doubled:
lighting one candle from another.

The Quickening: Mary's pregnancy at 16 weeks

If prayer is a bare tree,
clod-bound,
yet reaching up with jagged
branches to the boundless
pasture of sky,

think of her that day
his bare weight
reached the tipping point

and she could feel him beat
against the thickening
of her flesh,
fleeting as a silver-fish;

there-and-gone
as a firefly in the dusk.
It's a feeling as scarce
as your eyelash against
your cheek, the lightest spasm
of the eyelid

and she may have wondered
if it was so;
but there it was again.

That day, Christ in utero
found the softest
boundaries of the world,
and she knew,
in the newest sense,
the gravity-bound God

that swam; the first touch
of the divine to us.
That flickering in her womb,
was like buds on the stark branches
of our prayer;
in what seemed unending
silence: God's lips.

Ninth Month

Those heavy days, your lungs
squeezed breathless-high
by the child cramped
within you and girding his limbs,
Woman, what did you think?
Or was thought all prayer—trust
in this budding epiphany,
and the unquantifiable
blood to be let? But Mother,
those swollen days (olives clustering
in ashen leaves, or maybe new
wine leeching out its vinegar smell)
did you feel the tug of split hearts
in future cities, at tabernacles,
in bars? As your belly drew down
did you weigh, too, the clumsy imploring
down all our bloodlines
for this saving parcel of flesh?

She contains you
but not the thought of you.
She is like the firefly,
her skin so thin
she shows all that burns
and promises within.

Incarnation

From the remotest dawn, from a yellow eye,
sharper than the eagle's, that sees each one of us
scuttling in the shadow of a protective wing,
he falls to Earth—blind. Those first nights
the short distance between her breast and face
is as far as he can see. She is his first sight
of the world as man—our one pure sign.
She only knows his Christ-eyes latching
onto hers as fiercely as his gums clamp down
for milk. The future scrabbles, gnaws like rats
through a barn's corners and its eaves.
But she is transfixed by his skin and insistence
on her as the only visible, only beautiful thing—
the present moment; this is the first lesson of prayer.

Song for the Newborn Christ

Heavy the cold air,
gorgeous-heavy her round arms.
Then, the pointillist creation
of her smells—her milk, her hair
(his own skin looses newborn scent:
an altar that exhales incense).
Thank God he's moored to her close voice;
her arms soak up the tremble
of his earth-struck limbs.
Oh tiny, fragile, stricken ears
pricked to hear the story's end—
My God, just let me love, she sings.

His Face

His body is swaddled head to foot,
but his face is a window: one small pool of light.
This nakedness, that even Adam would not cover,
is a tender dish of listening, hunger
in the nuzzling nose and petal mouth, a sense
of all in the here and now—and dizzy distance,
like that one star announcing the expanse
of night. Lady, see the depths of his dark eyes.
This locked gaze is what keeps God and man
together. It is true prayer: he holding fast
to your face like a constellated sky; you tumbling
softly into him with no lights but those eyes.

To Saint Joseph, Listening to a Blackbird

For you, there will have been those wakeful nights
when it seemed as though creation had not happened,
or everything had already come to pass,
when one bird poured out a song of liquid glass,
heightening the emptiness and silence.
You listened, as your wife slept, heavy
and ready to break. You heard it when the child
was born and grown and slept near you in a safe
and hidden house. You heard the song and must
have known it was the child's that broke the vast,
and unlit space between yourself and God.
You did not live to see him die and resurrect.
The essence of his life as you kept vigil at his bed
was in this song, with its tone like silken oil,
that was louder than the world, and small.

The Prophetess Sees the Christ Child

She did not depart from the temple…
And coming up at that very hour
she gave thanks to God,
and spoke of him to all… (*Luke 2: 37, 38*)

I sing praise—billowing, heady—
as though juggling torches of flame.
In the tight dark of fasting and prayer,
I was earth-bound like a seed, feeding
on waiting and the close art of listening,
my cloistered flesh white as a tooth
in the night of a mouth. Then this:
the coming of him in luminous flesh
in her arms.
             I dreamed him in darkness,
see him now, and will see him again.
Words push up past my tongue—
I am old, but a reckless lover
of certainty: yes, his were the veins
nourished the black earth of my vigil:
I sing praise.

The Rightness of the Child

A soft crazing of white blossoms
makes sense of the bald sky.
Look how his baby skin glows
as he lies in your arms, watching them—
like a lantern of apricot or plum
in a tree's dark realm.

He unfurled within you, and now
he unfurls in your arms
until he can walk far away.
As a wild cherry is espaliered
against its own wayward growth,
he will only be stopped
on the black agony of a cross.

I wonder how much you wondered
about that brute ending. Or do you,
like any mother, consider all
questions settled
in eyelashes fretted
on his sleeping cheek;
in the shine of his skin;
in the uncanny command
of his faultless blossoming?

I walk on dry leaves.
A little boy collects them
like dropped pages.
It's evening. All I can do
is give everything to you.
Lime trees throw down
their long shadows
in exhausted adoration.

Magdalene: Washing His Feet

I take his feet, flesh closest to earth,
with their sigh of heat, blisters,
the cuts and aches. I wash, kiss him,
lift a piece of his pain and am gifted
with new doors flung open—
eye-bruising light in the soul's barn-dark.
There's noise overhead—
chewing of meat, talk,
clanking of cups—but here I am,
the peg pulling divinity down.

Only I know the quiet roar of touch,
the march of his being into myself.
As though I were a lily, and he
the water filling all of my veins.

Your Mother, Outside Asking for You

And a crowd was sitting about him; and they said to him,
"Your mother and your brethren
are outside, asking for you." And he replied,
"Who are my mother and my brethren?" (Mark 3, 32–33)

Outside, the soft bells of acacia trees
are lemon against blue, and inside the talk
mixes, thickens, congeals to a muscled
body of noise—one voice parting them
like a walker through wheat.
Out in the cold, yours is the un-let-loose
note that, solitary, would reach beyond
acres of sky. Your boy's deep inside;
yet you're with him—standing
on a street like a beggar, asking for God.

Woman that he filled, he needs you to know:
the boundary of flesh, the wall, the agony
of the impassable window. The burning
through your being as you make out your name.

A pane of glass catches
drops of rain—paralyzed
they shine, reflect
in miniature, like little eyes,
the tugged palm trees
and struggling sea.
            Be still,
you say, your hand like glass,
my heart open on the silent
wind-torn world.

The Bleeding Woman

I knew he was there by what surged around him,
as though he were the eye of a great wind,
and column-like in his stillness: no one else
was heavy enough to be steady in that street.
The nearer I got I sensed him like we sense
the sea yards from the shore, in the air's salty witness,
its unearthly chill. And nearer still, I knew a silence,
a weight, like the sunken stillness of burnt fields,
and nearer still, his hem was an edge like the draw
of a wave that I couldn't refuse. My God,
it was warm as an open wound and when he turned
I caught the deep, tumbling well of his gaze. My Christ
I knew then that prayer is all touch: the staunching
of his flesh on my losses, the merciful weakness of sky.

It's raining. No matter.
We walk till our skulls
are drenched and our coats
smell of the sheep
from which they came.
We talk of you; there is nothing
we talk more of these days.
There is no one in the street.
Birdsong comes effortlessly
through holes in the rain.

Peter: The Transfiguration

Tell no one, he said, for the structure of light
was like nothing before, and we had no words
to describe the taste, sound and sight
of that showering upon him. Our faces hugged
dirt. We were not ready to see, had not the mouths
to tell, the piercing joy that this white sun
foreshadowed. We fell down like bricks
with the burden of knowledge mute in our chests,
and not ready for any coherent unpacking.
And yet, in his movement and being and breath,
we stagger on—and yes, we're still finding flecks
of that light in the cupped hands of our prayer,
like refracted light in a river's dark muck—
a clarity that no words can bear.

Mary of Bethany: The Raising of Lazarus

A dead body thickens
to rock, then shrinks to something
like a washbowl or a chair in a room,
and unravels its losses in the stench
of cabbage, gut and vanilla.
But when he called me to the tomb
there was no smell at all,
and my sore eyes were stuffed
with dark's violet bruises
so I squinted to see my dead brother
walk out—the miracle
was his liquid lightness,
the soul pouring back through the body
(I felt it, now, in my own taut spine;
my blood and bones
pricked with layer on layer
of flight),
           —and the tight shroud
pulled off him in soft petal pieces.
Look at his face: dazed as a newborn,
blinded with distance. My bones
drew dark. The men chattered and spun.
These things can't be: like the moon
passing in front of the sun

and all our flesh and fear and being
let loose. The teacher turned
past the cacti and their prickly red fruit.
My brother and sister stumbled
back to the house. But I followed him,
punch-drunk, my body a scorched vessel,
choking to comprehend joy.

Like the cuckoo's hoarse cry
through a tangle of trees,
the thought of you
always escapes me.
But let it be snared
and held by these branches,
like a ruined kite,
a pulled tuft of hair.

Gethsemane

I watch the push of soft red petal from the cactus' tip,
the sticky cobweb strung from spike to spike.
These days, when prayer's too hoarse, too ripped
for words—I cannot say a word—does that still count?
Answer: we know how his tight mesh of skin that night
leaked drops of blood. And how the angel came,
pushed through the dark like hand through sleeve,
like notes of ordered song from vicious wind. All comes
from inside out. Dread thoughts escape, un-skinned,
and wild—like moths or silver flash of olive leaves—
but, too, the angel comes from where he hid, and sings.
The curtain tears and so does skin and so does prayer.
It is a kind of wordless tearing—our brokenness used
as entry for him; our brokenness filled by his.

Veronica

Even the yellow sun was out of tune—
humming to itself, indifferent.
The dust flew up and choked,
burnt the blood in open wounds.
Some were sad, some shook their head for shame.
But the demonic symphony of shouts,
the tearing of the ragged flesh,
were conductor-less, un-reined,
and grew like some escaping thing
that crushes as it runs—thought, horizons, men—
and feeds on what it breaks.

She put a hand through all of that—
a cloth that soaked up a fraction
of the weight of blood and sweat.

I imagine that for seconds
the racket stilled; even pain
skipped its chaotic, syncopated beat.
The gentle pressure of her touch
was magnified by its perfect
pitch of love, in the same way
one true note chimes smoothly
through our bones and skin,
and rises up in us, as though
it's part of us and him,
as though it's also we who sing.

The Crucifier

As I nailed him I deafened myself
to the shafting of steel through taut wires
of tendons, through flesh, past black pain
that snuffed out all thought. Did I look
into the bottomless eyes and whisper
I was sorry—or did all that come later?
Did I let my gaze feed on the faraway hills?
The women's crescendo of cries
made me go faster: I hammered with duty
and tiredness, and waited as dark fell
on the cross. But in my dreams I'm still
hammering, deaf, as wind turns the world
over, and I hammer harder, knowing I forge
the one still point—like the solderer beating
the whitest hot metal, I'm crafting the fulcrum
where God's melded with us in our unbending
rage—and if I could, in this chaos,
I would set all my children safe upon the crux
of that nail. O my God, how can I bear it:
chosen to be the necessary hurter?
I pray to what slipped away in the long grass
of our silence—that all I was flipped
to goodness on the head of a nail.

The Mother (i)

A man once hypothesized that Mary ran from the Cross
to save her own skin. Surely he was blind to these things:
Christ as a blasted tree, fused black against the sky--
scourged, slashed, stabbed-- and his mother as the deep roots
beneath him. How could she go? She was the earthed
wire of his agony, routing his pain to the earth's marrow:
the ground will never stop singing, nor our bones,
if they'll listen. Our children hurt and they cry;
we carry their grief in our frames like a new
kind of gravity. Understand, you who doubt this love,
or the grit to bear it: the long fields are ready for running,
and many do run. But like those fields seeded thoroughly
with yellow everlastings, she is the ground of his life,
the shell of his sounding. There is nowhere else she could be.

Silence

The Mother (ii)

She stands in darkness. The groaning
within her is more than flooding
or thunder: if they heard it
it would shatter their ears.
She stands and grieves to the dark;
the earth breaks into pieces.
Her heart gives: a web of cracks
running through it like the crazing
of china. But—as though each
split were a vessel interlocked
with another—it does not fall apart.

Holy Saturday

This is the way of man: to gather up the body and shut it in,
and try, uselessly, to go back to the way things were again.

The earth is blood-logged. Blood feeds each thoughtless weed.
In dark houses, women's ears are strummed by those last cries;

sounds that will not die, and have come to shape them
as dry trees are cupped around the cry of long-spent wind.

The light is strange, says one, and the road is dull to the feet;
as though a covering had been drawn across the sky.

The Body in the Tomb

To be sure, the tomb was sealed that day.
The garden struggled to swallow the rain.
Inside, his skin was cool, not hard.
Ants wound a path around long fingers,
but flesh was too tight for maggot eggs
and no rat smelt a scent. The tomb
was not built for such a quiet occupant,
incorruptible sleeper, who was with a thief
in paradise and with the reams of dead
in Hades. His blood pooled and steadied
as though after a long storm, but without
letting drop the grit of slow black sediment.

Three days on, he collected his body
like a best possession, as though
thoughts were knit in each commonplace toe;
as though liver, duodenum, held messages:
smell of chrysanthemum a woman
laid in with him; psalms known to the bone;
taste of a night's shuddering dread. He rose,
we're told. Flesh, the rain-logged garden
breathed; what we do well not to forget.

The Testimony of Mary Magdalene

First light shivered; the men departed.
I went to him to cradle his head,
to scent his skin with myrrh and nard,
to take the coins from his deep eyes
and a portion of his pain in my hands.
But the guardians of absence spoke of him
like rings in a pond, and I longed
for his flesh in the dawn of this hunger.

Woman, why are you weeping?

They wrote I thought he was the gardener.
It was only me clutching at the possible.
I could not pick the words to tell—
and still can't. It was like
dark white
        like a white house bursting
blackly with brightness
when you go in out of the sun.

Or, no:

It was like seeing myself stand beside me,
like a rock to the skull,
I almost fell.

Or, no:

It was God

beside me and new knowledge
mushroomed deep in my bones.
The rock roses bloomed and I knew
the draw of each petal,
the silence of each stone.

Dumbly, I reached out to touch.

His presence lay on my tongue
like a new language
I was learning to speak.
Real love comes to this:
the death of everything else.

Last night, a restless wind—
every doorway howled and ached.
This morning you returned,
like stillness.
            Now the pines
are spent; there's not a breath.
Only this hunger as I reach out
to touch you; only this longing.

Mary's Resurrection

Somewhere in the inkwell of that night,
or the shaken clarity of morning
there was a moment that you *knew* his rising,
and though faith may have led you to expect it,
there's a difference between the shimmering lit
shadow-rings beside a glass of water,
and the drink itself. Where were you, Mother,

when you knew? Did the swords slide cleanly
from your heart? The tight and gritty shadows
of a mother's pain that intimately and silently
mark each step of her child's agony
and graft it deep into her own heart's wall—
did all this fall from you in one gifted
moment, or as you ran to meet him?

Or was there a sudden doubling in you:
the knowledge of God's plan coupling with each
crazed memory—not canceling, but telling
you that each hair of every head is known;
each suffering is dancing with this Love?
See how the pain rises, like vapor from the fields,
its broken scent escaping—you too are lifted.

Here is stillness
(the trees are mute,
wind laid down like cloth).
In one small breath
I give up will and words.

I can see nothing
but your naked feet.
and step up on them
as I used to on
my granddad's shoes,
to be wheeled and danced
around a room.

In prayer's dark wood,
unthinking
as a leaf that's cradled down
through tilting steps of air,
I'm borne on you—

rapt, in dance,
in darkness;
no words but you,
in flesh and here and now,
and me full-here,
blind to all but you,
as I almost never am.

The Blooding

Scarlet berries by the hundred break
quietly, violently, the green-black leaves—
like drops of Blood, our fathers used to say—
and late sun floods and reddens snow.
The world's never got over the darkening
of your death—all nature dimmed and kneeled
at the slowing of your blood; earth plates
dislocated at the wrenching of your breath.
Birds hushed. But even now, your Cross
is everywhere: at the tops of wooden poles,
in the fall of bindweed in long grasses.
Each moment is inscribed with you—
unspeakable loss, desire. In prayer
I fall further into you: your gaze cave-deep,
a plummeting mine. Your love gallops
through the earth, through me—even now
it won't turn back—; it lives again, it protects.
And like a child on his first hunt whose cheek
is brushed with the slaughtered fox's tail,
all of creation has been blooded.

Our feet are dead with cold,
our hands too numb to hold
in prayer. Our white breath
sinks. For what would we pray?
To be able to pray, to know
your presence, the falling down
and through us like rain.
In the chapel, there is a bank
of tiny votive flames,
(their light ripples like a field of corn)
and through their liquid haze,
an icon of your living face.

A Norfolk Christmas

My father didn't believe. Together we looked
over the corner where he'd lie: stark lungs
of winter trees, the blank, no-nonsense altar
of flat fields, and peace, he said. This Christmas,
rabbits eat the roses on my father's grave
and every blade of grass is clamped by frost.
The Saxon church, so old and emptied-out
its grey bones can't be still, shudders echoes
as I walk inside. But listen: tonight,
under the dark lid of sky, God is flesh,
and his mother guards him like a lioness.
She won't sleep now. Her hours of prayer
are upside down: the ineffable, infinite
God tucked into her neck; the bloody world
crouched invisible outside. Here, now,
her flesh is his country; her face is his home.
And from that touch of God's blood to this earth,
here, still stitched into everything, he *is*.
The grey stone church burns with cold. Fog rises
from the fields like desert heat or incense.
And the stripped branches above my father's grave
are a tangle of many waiting crosses.

No one in church.
Pews damp with cold,

smeared with fingerprints.
In the altar's light I kneel

and you unfold through me
like arms of branches

defining a lost sky.

The Hermit

He can't see the iodine split
from broken waves,
and sucked into the straits

of his lungs. Indeed, high
on his hillside, the sea
has the sheer fabric

of another earth,
and air's so still he almost knows
its interstices—

like honeycomb,
or the wordless edges
around thought.

Listen: a dropped pin would sing,
and does.
A mouse twitters through the garden.

But they are only here to aver
stillness, as God
avers himself in vacancy.

Listen: the air's agape with prayer
and song, the tasks
of knowing—

when nothing is left to be taken
or plundered
but the pure pipes of air

yielding notes;
but the narrow veins of air
birthing, in time,

his homeland,
the inexpressible bodies
of his angels.

Three Hares

In the still, blue snow the hare's eye is steady as God's,
and dark. His veined ear is tuned
to the anticipation of sound,
and the hermitage's silence;
its one light burning. Stripped trees;
the cold smell of nothing—and then, from nowhere,
two more hares complete the steady gaze
of a trinity. Their fur is white now,
changed, as though this freeze brought on grief
and they surrendered to its will with agility.
Their ears are not shells shaped for noise,
but bodies offered up to the moment:
sensitive, secret, stung.
We pray our souls are so Christ-like:
nakedly attending; and that we may absorb,
as these hares do the morning,
the great breath of the Word.

The Dream

When she woke me, the dream, in its broken heat,
its loud and private noise, drew up to sight,
still hot and beating blood, like a lamb just slaughtered:
I was at the altar, so near to him there was no need
to take, eat; I felt his warmth I was that close,
and it drenched me; I was suspended like an embryo
in his snug and rightful sea.
I drew my daughter into bed when she walked in
(without her the dream would've stayed unknown),
and her small head leant on mine,
the dream still golden, saturating my head:
such joy that I could transmit it to her, like heat,
and joy because, for that night at least,
my dream and what lies within me, always, were one.

I searched for you all day,
in books, down streets,
in silence's fretful woods.
It wasn't till I slept
and half-awoke
that I sensed you there
under the lip of sleep,
powering me, the room,
the vast, un-ignorable sky.
You were louder, more colorful
than dreams, easier
to find than my own hands;
a tale I was caught up in,
long, long underway.

About the Author

SALLY READ has published three collections of poetry with Bloodaxe Books. Her 2010 conversion to Catholicism is recounted in *Night's Bright Darkness*, which was followed by *Annunciation, a Call to Faith in a Broken World*. Her work has been translated into five languages, and her articles have appeared in *The Times Literary Supplement* and *The Tablet*. She hosted Radio Maria England's *Poetry for the Season*, and since 2020 has been poet in residence of the Hermitage of the Three Holy Hierarchs. She lives in Rome, Italy with her family. More about her can be found at www.sallyread.net.

Made in the USA
Monee, IL
07 February 2024

53089485R00042